ILLUMINATION PRESENTS

THE SECRET LIFE OF Pets

ANNUAL 2017

THIS ANNUAL **BELONGS TO:**

centum

HOW MANY TIMES CAN YOU FIND DRAGON HIDDEN IN THIS BOOK?

CONTENTS

MEET MAX!

MAX is the most loyal mutt in Manhattan. He lives for his owner, Katie, and their perfect world together. Perfect, that is, until Duke shows up!

FACT FILE

NAME: Max

LIKES: Being with Katie

BREED: Terrier mix

DISLIKES: Not being with Katie
And big hairy bed-stealers.

BIGGEST ACHIEVEMENT:
Spending a whole day on the rug by the front door waiting for Katie to come home.

DUKE TIME!

DUKE is big, hairy and not so fond of personal hygiene. He's just trying to make the best of life, even if that means making an enemy of Max.

FACT FILE

NAME: Duke

BREED: Cross

LIKES: Food and snuggly dog beds

DISLIKES: Empty food bowls and whiny terriers

BIGGEST ACHIEVEMENT:
Eating an entire pack of jumbo wieners without removing the wrapper.

MEET GIDGET!

Being a pampered pooch doesn't automatically mean you'll be super-happy. All GIDGET really wants in life is to be noticed by her neighbour . . .

NAME: Gidget

LIKES: Max ... a lot!

BIGGEST ACHIEVEMENT:
Getting Max to talk to her at least once a day.

BREED: Pomeranian

DISLIKES: Not being noticed by Max.

FACT FILE

MEET CHLOE!

Let's just say that if you plan on visiting CHLOE, make sure you bring a treat, or twelve. This kitty doesn't get out of bed for less than a full roast chicken.

NAME: Chloe

LIKES: Food. Food. Food.

BIGGEST ACHIEVEMENT: Never getting full.

BREED: Cat

DISLIKES: Boring, dry cat food.

FACT FILE

11

MEET MEL!

MEL is the kind of pug that will always cheer you up and make you laugh, even if he doesn't always know why you are laughing . . .

FACT FILE

NAME: Mel

BREED: Pug

LIKES: His pink cushion

DISLIKES: Squirrels

BIGGEST ACHIEVEMENT:
Keeping the tree outside his window free from vermin (otherwise known as squirrels).

MEET BUDDY!

BUDDY is a pleasure-seeking pooch – get ready to meet him!

FACT FILE

NAME: Buddy

BREED: Dachshund

LIKES: Massages

DISLIKES: Squirrels. Especially those taller than him.

BIGGEST ACHIEVEMENT:
Being the first to spot butterflies in the park.

13

MEET SWEETPEA AND TIBERIUS

FACT FILE

NAME: Sweetpea

BREED: Budgie

LIKES: Flight training

DISLIKES: Being caged in.

BIGGEST ACHIEVEMENT:
Completing video games before his owner.

FACT FILE

NAME: Tiberius

BREED: Hawk

LIKES: Small animals (to eat!)

DISLIKES: Being lonely.

BIGGEST ACHIEVEMENT:
Having the sharpest claws on the block.

MEET NORMAN AND LEONARD

FACT FILE

NAME: Norman

BREED: Guinea Pig

LIKES: . . . he's forgotten!

DISLIKES: Anything too mentally challenging.

BIGGEST ACHIEVEMENT:
Not getting eaten by Tiberius.

FACT FILE

NAME: Leonard

BREED: Giant poodle

LIKES: Hard rock

DISLIKES: Not being adequately groomed.

BIGGEST ACHIEVEMENT:
Head-banging champion 2016.

WINDOW WATCHING

It's lights out in the apartment building, but can you still work out which Pet lives in each apartment? DRAW a line between the Pet and their apartment.

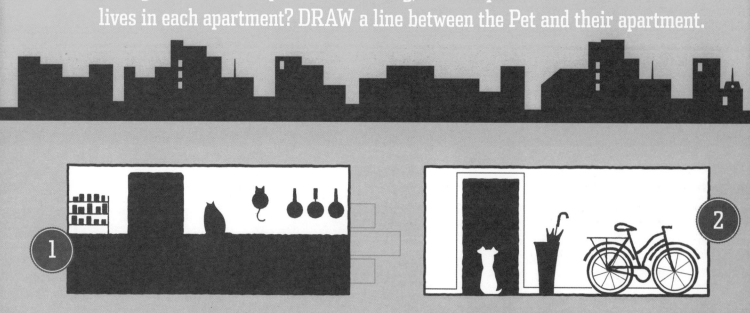

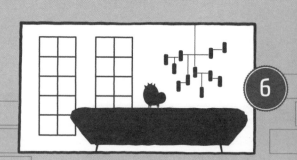

Sweetpea

Chloe

Gidget

Leonard

Max

Buddy

DINNER TIME

CHLOE's looking unimpressed with her supper, maybe she can find something tastier in the fridge? In the meantime, can you SPOT the six differences between these two pictures?

1

2

Answers on page 76

BIG LOVE

Read the descriptions then DRAW a line to match each Pet to its favourite thing in the whole world.

 1

MAX'S
favourite thing:
- Is called Katie
- Has dark hair
- Is Max's owner

 2

GIDGET'S
favourite thing:
- Wears a blue collar
- Is her neighbour
- Has brown ears

 3

LEONARD'S
favourite thing:
- Is full of rock songs
- Can play music loudly
- Has speakers

 4

MEL'S
favourite thing:
- Is called 'Doggie b...
- Can be eaten
- Is a snack

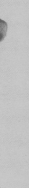

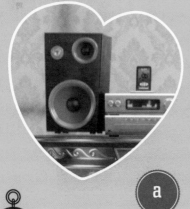 **a**

 **b**

 **c**

 **d**

WHAT'S MISSING?

Looks like Duke is going to be in big trouble! Find out just how much by matching up the missing pieces of the picture. Which piece DOESN'T fit?

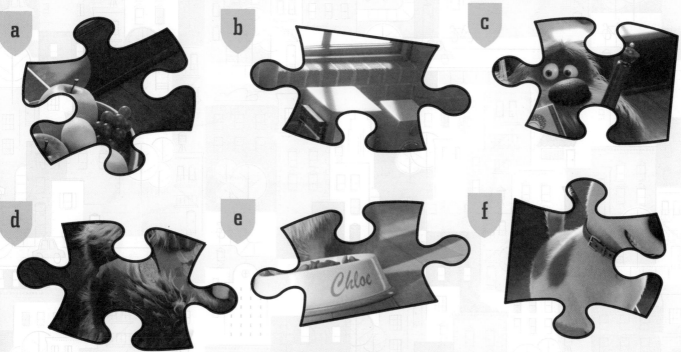

a

b

c

d

e

f

Answers on page 76

DRAW MAX

Use the guide below to DRAW Max in the big grid on the opposite page. When you've finished, COLOUR him in!

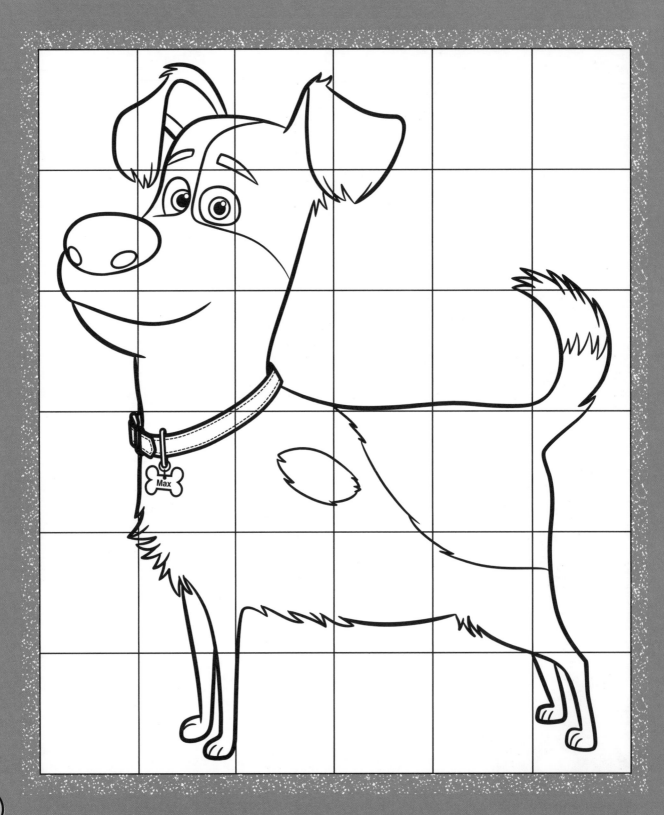

20

For Max, life was PERFECT. He lived in New York City with his owner, Katie. Max didn't think of Katie as his owner, they were more like best friends . . . or soul mates!

Every day Katie would take Max to the park in the basket of her bike and each evening they would snuggle up together on the sofa. Max loved his life with Katie, but there was one small thing he wanted to change . . .

Each day Katie left for a few hours and Max had no idea why! He'd try all his best tricks to convince her to stay, but she always left Max behind to wait for her until she returned. Luckily, Max wasn't completely alone. The building where Max and Katie lived was full of pets, all of which were also killing time before their owners got home.

Some of the pets liked to hang out in Max's apartment, including Gidget, the Pomeranian next door, whose favourite pastime was staring at Max.

"I've got big plans today, Gidget," said Max. "I'm going to sit here and wait until Katie gets back."

"That sounds exciting!" replied Gidget, happily.

Chloe, the grey food-loving cat from upstairs, thudded through the window followed by an excitable pug named Mel and a fearless bird called Sweetpea. The Pet friends whiled away the hours before returning home in time to greet their owners.

Max sighed happily as he thought about his perfect life. Soon he heard keys in the door and he jumped with delight – Katie was home!

"Now, I've got some BIG NEWS for you," Katie said, trying to keep the door from opening behind her. "This is Duke," Katie said as a giant, scruffy and very hairy dog bounded through the door. "He's going to be your new brother!"

MAX STARED AT THIS NEW CREATURE IN AMAZEMENT. WHAT WAS HE GOING TO DO NOW?

FUR-MAZING!

Take a look at the fabulous fur, then match it to the correct Pet.
WRITE the name of each pet when you've made a match!

Have a look through the book for CLUES.

1

2

3

4

5

Answers on page 76

WISH YOU
WERE HERE

FETCH

LIKE YOU
MEAN IT

WHO'S IN THE BED?

JOIN the DOTS to discover who has taken over Max's cosy basket!

Don't forget to COLOUR IN this cosy scene.

has taken over the bed!

CHLOE'S CUPCAKE CHALLENGE!

Can you FIND 17 cupcakes hidden in Chloe's apartment?

GLAMOROUS GIDGET

We're pretty sure Gidget would like all these bags, but can you work out which one is hers? MATCH each bag into pairs and find the odd one out to discover Gidget's real bag.

Answers on page 76

COLOUR IN CHLOE

FOODIE

31

Max couldn't believe what Katie had brought home! Did she expect them to share their home with a **BIG**, slobbering and hairy creature?!

As Katie kissed Max and Duke goodnight, Max grumpily headed for his nice comfy bed, shooting a 'stay away' look at Duke. Duke had his eyes on Max's comfy bed too.

"I'm sure we could both fit," Duke said with mock friendliness, before squeezing Max out onto the cold, hard floor.

Max couldn't take it any longer; he had to tell Katie how awful Duke really was.

The next morning, as Max furiously tried to talk to Katie, all Katie heard were barks! So, she left for work as usual, leaving Max alone with Duke. As Duke started to eat both bowls of food that Katie had left out for them, Norman, a lost hamster from another apartment, appeared through a vent in the wall.

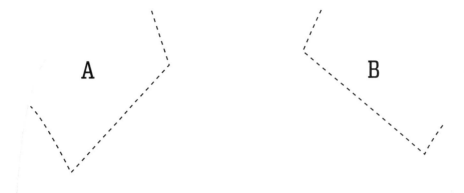

A

B

Glue the ears to the reverse of the
mask as indicated by the dotted
lines and labels. You'll find Max's
ears on Chloe's mask page.

MAX

DUKE

Carefully press-out the two halves of the Duke mask and stick them together.

DUKE

SNO W BALL

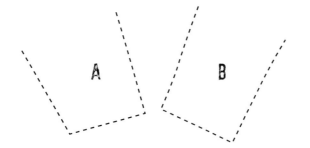

GLUE THE EARS TO THE REVERSE
OF THE MASK AS INDICATED BY THE
DOTTED LINES AND LABELS.

B

A

A   B

MAX'S
EARS

CHLOE

TM and © Universal Studios

Press out Duke and hold him in front of a camera while taking a photograph of your friends or yourself. Remember to hold the stand part of the image so that you can't see your fingers in the photo!

Duke growled and launched himself at the terrified Norman, knocking into a vase and sending it crashing to the floor. Suddenly, Max had an idea – he knew just how to get rid of Duke forever! Max started to SMASH other things around the apartment.

"What are you doing?" asked Duke in disbelief.

"Oh, nothing," replied Max, grinning. "I'm just a cute little doggy and Katie knows I wouldn't do anything like this!"

Duke understood. If he didn't do exactly what Max said, he'd make him look bad in front of Katie and his comfy new home would disappear.

Later that day, the dog walker arrived and took Max and Duke to the park. Max bossed Duke around with his new-found power, demanding that Duke find him the perfect stick. Soon Duke had had enough. When the dog walker was distracted he grabbed Max's lead and dragged him into a lonely alleyway and dumped him in a bin.

"No hard feelings, Max!" Duke laughed as he shut the lid. Before Duke had time to gloat, he discovered that the alley was full of mean alley cats, lead by the hairless and frightening Ozone. Duke fled, leaving Max to be tied up by the cats. When Duke came running back, Max thought he had come back to rescue him, but Duke was being chased by a bigger problem – **ANIMAL CONTROL!**

PET'S PARADISE

Can you FIND the names of all these
adored Pets in the grid below?

MAX • DUKE • BUDDY • MEL • SWEETPEA
GIDGET • LEONARD • CHLOE • NORMAN • POPS

S	D	F	R	T	G	H	Y	U	J	K	I	O	P
X	C	V	F	L	E	M	S	D	F	G	E	W	D
M	T	D	A	B	U	O	G	E	S	K	E	M	A
B	A	L	R	D	E	R	E	H	U	C	V	F	E
H	G	D	E	Q	W	E	R	D	V	B	H	D	T
F	G	H	J	O	S	A	W	E	R	S	P	O	P
D	F	G	H	B	N	A	S	D	F	G	H	J	K
H	G	F	D	D	W	A	C	V	B	N	G	J	U
V	B	G	X	C	D	S	R	A	E	R	Y	H	J
Y	T	I	W	D	B	N	H	D	T	D	Y	U	A
C	V	D	S	D	F	G	T	Y	D	J	K	L	E
M	V	G	C	V	D	F	G	U	R	G	N	M	P
A	E	E	J	N	J	K	B	W	E	R	G	N	T
X	D	T	C	G	H	B	Y	F	U	I	V	B	E
F	C	T	W	D	F	C	V	G	H	J	F	C	E
C	V	R	W	S	C	H	L	O	E	U	R	B	W
H	G	F	F	D	F	G	T	Y	H	J	E	B	S
N	O	R	M	A	N	V	B	G	Y	T	W	F	E

34

WATCH OUT, MAX!

Looks like Max has got himself into a tight spot! Can you SPOT the six differences between the two pictures?

1

2

COMPLETE
PET PERFECTION

Complete the grid by making sure each pet only appears once in each row and column. DRAW the characters in place, or just WRITE in their name!

FEELING FLUSHED?

DRAW EACH **FLUSHED PET** ONCE INTO EACH ROW AND COLUMN.

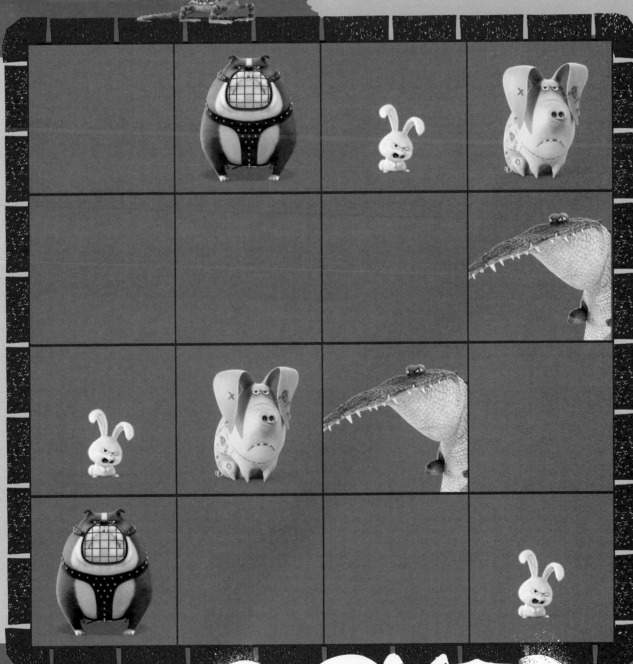

LIBERATED FOREVER! DOMESTICATED NEVER!

ANSWERS ON PAGE 77

WHICH PET ARE YOU?

Answer the QUESTIONS, add up your answers and find out which pet is your **ANIMAL SOULMATE!**

What's your friendship group like?

a I have one very special friend and we do everything together.

b I have a few friends, but I like making new friends when I can.

c Everyone loves me. What's not to love?

d I can take or leave human company.

What's your beauty regime?

a I like to look nice for the people around me.

b I get up extra early and make sure my hair is perfect.

You never know who you might meet!

c What's a beauty regime?

d I am what I eat.

What's your favourite type of food?

a Whatever I can share with family and friends.

b Anything served on a silver platter.

c I'm quite fond of sausages . . .

d Anything delicious.

Can you keep a secret?

a Totally! I'm 100% honest and loyal.

b Yes, although I don't have many.

c Sometimes.

d Yes. Unless I can swap the secret for food.

When are you happiest?

a Playing with my best friend.

b Chatting with pals.

c Sleeping. Or Eating. Or both.

d When the fridge is full.

Mostly As: Max!

You are loyal, trustworthy and would do anything for the people you love. You're not great at sharing your special things and you like to stick to the rules!

Mostly Bs: Gidget!

You are kind and brave, just like Gidget! You like the finer things in life and keep yourself looking spotless.

Mostly Cs: Duke!

You throw yourself into anything and like to find the best in any situation. You might not have the best grooming regime, but people love you regardless.

Mostly Ds: Chloe

So, basically, if was a choice between people and food, you'd choose food. Every time.

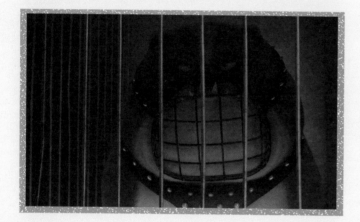

MAX AND DUKE WERE IN TROUBLE.
BIG TROUBLE. They had just narrowly escaped from a group of maniac alley cats, but now they were face-to-face with two guys from Animal Control and their nets. Both dogs were scooped up and placed inside cages in the back of a van. The only other animal inside was a squat bulldog called Ripper. Ripper didn't say much. He preferred to keep himself busy by banging his head against the side of the van.

What Max and Duke didn't know was that Ripper's head-banging had a purpose. Just below the surface of the road, a small, white, fluffy rabbit called Snowball was heading above ground. The Animal Control van stopped and picked up the seemingly cute bunny – but Snowball was anything but cute! In a flash, he had overpowered the guys from Animal Control, allowing his accomplices (a pig called Tattoo and a lizard called Dragon) to take over the van.

Snowball soon found Ripper and freed him from his cage using a key made out of a carrot. Dragon and Tattoo were trying to drive the van, but being a pig and lizard, they soon crashed – leaving Max and Duke trapped inside their locked cages.

Max knew that the only way out of their cages was to join this gang of crazy creatures, who called themselves

'The Flushed Pets'.

"Hey! Take us with you!" cried Max.

"I don't think so, Pets," replied Snowball, about to eat his carrot key. "You've got the stench of domestication all over you!"

Max was desperate to be freed from his cage.

"WE HATE HUMANS!" he said.

"Yeah and we killed our owners!" said Duke, joining in. This was good enough for Snowball. He released Duke and Max and told them they were now part of the Flushed Pets. Max and Duke nodded and followed Snowball, Ripper, Tattoo and Dragon back to their underground hideout in the sewers.

Back at the apartment, Gidget had noticed that Max was missing. Gidget was madly in love with Max and so she decided she had to be the one to find him. She made a daring dash out of her apartment window and headed for the roof. She was sure that she would see him from there!

Even with her little legs, she was determined and made it all the way to the roof, where she met a pet hawk named Tiberius. Gidget, being a trusting little dog, agreed to release Tiberius as long as he helped her to look for Max. At first, Tiberius only saw Gidget as a tasty snack, but when Gidget promised to be his best friend, lonely Tiberius agreed to help her.

WATCH OUT, THIS BUNNY BITES!

GREATEST ACHIEVEMENT:
BEING AN UNDERGROUND MASTERMIND AND BUNNY ON THE RUN.

NAME: SNOWBALL

ANIMAL: RABBIT

LIKES: BUSTING ANIMALS OUT OF ANIMAL CONTROL

DISLIKES: OWNERS

THIS KITTY IS UGLY ON THE OUTSIDE ... AND THE INSIDE.

NAME: OZONE

ANIMAL: CAT

LIKES: BEING TOP ALLEYCAT AND GETTING HIS OWN WAY

DISLIKES: DOGS

WHO YOU CALLING PORK CHOP?

NAME: TATTOO

BREED: POT-BELLIED PIG

LIKES: DRIVING, RECKLESSLY

DISLIKES: WHEN HIS OWNER USED TO PRACTISE DRAWING TATTOOS ON HIM.

MEET DERICK, DRAGON AND RIPPER

NAME:	DERICK
ANIMAL:	CROCODILE
LIKES:	PROTECTING SNOWBALL

NAME: DRAGON
BREED: BEARDED DRAGON
LIKES: CLIMBING UP WALLS
          AND ACROSS CEILINGS

NAME: RIPPER
BREED: BULLDOG
LIKES: SCARING PEOPLE
          AND OTHER ANIMALS
DISLIKES: THE DOG POUND

CLIMBING NEW HEIGHTS

HELP Gidget through the maze to get to Tiberius. Make sure she picks up the rest of the Pets on the way!

Answers on page 77

I DON'T GET *Out much*

TM & © UNI

Unimpressed

MATCH THE SHADOW

These pets are trying to sneak around without being seen! MATCH each shadow to the Pets.

1

a

2

b

c

d

3

4

Answers on page 77

DRAW GIDGET

Use the guide below to DRAW Gidget in the big grid on the opposite page. When you've finished, COLOUR her in!

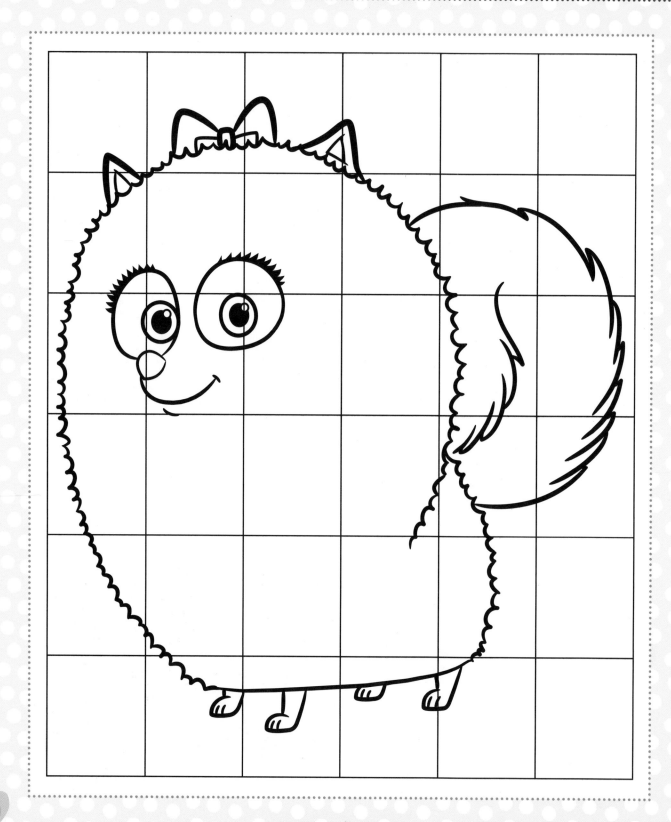

Deep underground, Max and Duke had been taken to the Flushed Pets' secret hideout, the Underbelly.

"It's time for your initiation!" cried Snowball.

Snowball proudly introduced Max and Duke to the rest of his gang, before opening a large grate to reveal a large, blind, one-fanged viper.

"EACH OF YOU MUST BE BITTEN BY THE VIPER TO BECOME A TRUE FLUSHED PET!"

There was no way Max or Duke wanted to be bitten by the viper, but they couldn't see a way out. As the viper opened its huge jaws, Nitro, a cat from the alleyway, appeared.

"Why are you initiating pets?" Nitro cried.

Nitro revealed that Max and Duke weren't owner-killing rebels at all; they were pets! Snowball was furious! The Flushed Pets started to chase Max and Duke out of the sewers.

"YOU DON'T DESERVE TO BE BITTEN BY THE VIPER!" SNOWBALL RAGED. "YOU DESERVE TO BE EATEN BY HIM!"

Meanwhile, back at the apartment block, Tiberius had found Ozone and delivered him to Gidget. Ozone coughed up Max's collar and, after some gentle persuasion from Gidget, he revealed that Max and Duke had been taken to the sewers.

Gidget was terrified. She had to save Max but she needed help, it was time to gather the apartment pets.

Unaware of Gidget's rescue plan, Max and Duke had fled down a pipe. At the end of the pipe there was a long drop into some disgusting sewage. The Flushed Pets were on their tail and they had no choice but to take leap into the sludge.

Free from the Flushed Pets, Max and Duke floated in the sewage until they found themselves in the East River. Duke spotted a boat and he managed to climb on board. He threw a life ring to Max and helped him to safety.

"AT LAST!" GASPED MAX. "I'M GOING HOME!"

But Duke knew better. "Um, isn't home that way?" he said as Max realised the boat was heading in the opposite direction from home!

WHICH FLUSHED PET ARE YOU?

ANSWER THE QUESTIONS, TOTAL UP YOUR ANSWERS AND SEE WHICH FLUSHED PET IS YOUR CREEPY COMPANION.

SOMEONE JUST TOOK THE LAST CHOCOLATE CHIP COOKIE. WHAT DO YOU DO?

1

- **A** NOTHING YET. YOU NEED TIME TO PLOT YOUR REVENGE.
- **B** NO ONE WOULD DARE DO THAT IN FRONT OF YOU!
- **C** PESTER THEM INTO GIVING IT TO YOU.

WHAT'S YOUR PERSONALITY?

2

- **A** LOUD AND OUTGOING.
- **B** QUIET AND THOUGHTFUL.
- **C** CALM AND CUNNING.

WHO'S YOUR IDEAL FRIEND?

3

A SOMEONE WHO DOES WHATEVER I SAY.

B SOMEONE AS BRAVE AS ME.

C SOMEONE WHO'LL TELL ME WHAT TO DO.

WHAT'S YOUR FAVOURITE FOOD?

4

A CRUNCHY SALAD.

B STEAK.

C FISH.

WHEN ARE YOU HAPPIEST?

5

A LEADING A GROUP, PREFERABLY SHOUTING AT THE SAME TIME.

B EATING.

C MAKING MISCHIEF.

MOSTLY AS SNOWBALL!

AS THE LEADER OF THE FLUSHED PETS YOU AND SNOWBALL HAVE A LOT IN COMMON. YOU LIKE TO GET YOUR OWN WAY AND WILL FIGHT FOR ANYTHING YOU BELIEVE IN.

MOSTLY BS RIPPER!

HE DOESN'T SAY MUCH, BUT RIPPER DOESN'T HAVE TO! YOU MAY BE QUIET, BUT THAT DOESN'T MEAN YOU'RE A PUSHOVER. PEOPLE BETTER NOT PUSH YOU, OR YOU MIGHT UNLEASH YOUR BARK!

MOSTLY CS OZONE!

YOU'RE THE CUNNING CAT WHO, LIKE OZONE, WILL FOLLOW EXCITING PLANS AS LONG AS THEY BENEFIT YOU! YOU MIGHT NOT SHOUT ABOUT IT, BUT YOU LIKE TO GET YOUR OWN WAY.

SUPPER TIME!

Duke wants to sit at the end of the conveyer belt with the most sausages.

Which one should he CHOOSE? _____

a   b   c   d   e

Answers on page 77

GOING UNDERGROUND

CAN YOU FIT THE NAMES OF EACH OF THESE WORDS ONTO THE GRID? EACH WORD ONLY FITS INTO THE GRID IN ONE PLACE, SO COUNT THE LETTERS OF EACH WORD CAREFULLY.

◉ SNOWBALL ◉ TATTOO ◉ DRAGON ◉ DERICK
◉ RIPPER ◉ OZONE ◉ FLUSHED ◉ PETS ◉ SEWER

ODD TATTOO OUT

TAKE A CLOSE LOOK AT TATTOO THEN SEE IF YOU CAN SPOT THE **TATTOO BELOW** WHICH **DOESN'T** MATCH PERFECTLY.

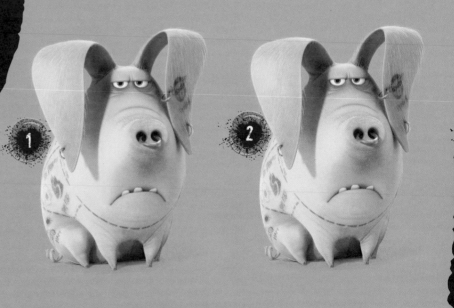

1

2

ANSWERS ON PAGE 77

3

4

5

WASHING LINE SCRAMBLE!

Will YOU be the first to make it to the top?

How to play:

Find two counters and place them at the bottom of the alley.

Now pop a pencil on the wheel and take it in turns to spin.

Move your counter to the nearest type of clothing matching the picture you land on. You can move upwards and sideways only.

The first player to reach the top washing line is the winner!

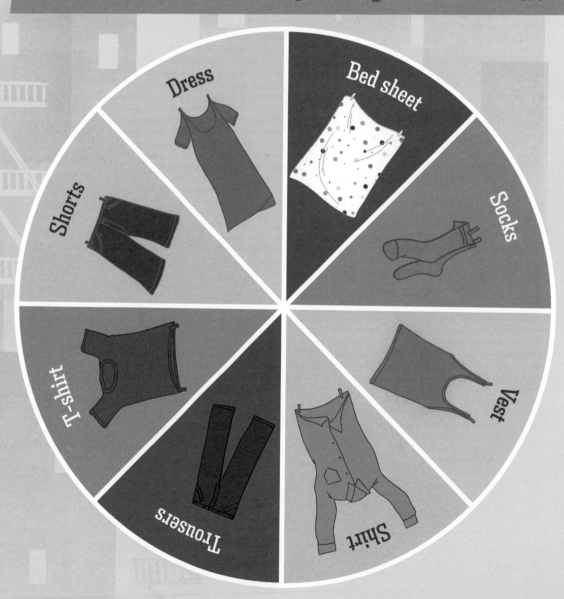

FINISH

START

61

Gidget had gathered the apartment pets together to help her look for Max, including Chloe, Mel, Sweetpea, Norman and a dachshund named Buddy. Buddy said he knew a dog called Pops who knew everyone in the city, so the group of unlikely heroes went to Pops' apartment.

Pops' place was full of pets having the time of their lives.

"Pops' owner is never home," explained Buddy as he lead the pets over to an old sleeping dog in the corner of the room. His back legs were mounted on wheels and the pets didn't think that Pops looked like he was going to be able to help . . .

But Gidget was desperate to find Max and pleaded with Pops to help.

"I know someone in the sewers," Pops said. "Follow me."

Meanwhile, Max and Duke's boat had finally come to a stop and they jumped out onto dry land. They were both hungry and exhausted and luckily, at that moment, Duke's smelt something delicious on the wind.

"SAUSAGES!" he cried, as Max smelt it too! The two dogs followed the scent and rushed into a sausage factory and leapt, paws first, into a huge pile of scrumptious sausages.

Back in New York, Pops was leading the pets around the secret passageways of the city and then down into the sewers. Finally, the pets discovered that Pops was looking for Viper! Instead, they came across Snowball and the Flushed Pets who were planning their revenge on Max and Duke.

In the sausage factory Duke told Max that he used to have an owner, but that one day he got lost and was taken in by Animal Control. Max couldn't believe that this hairy beast once had a life just like his and Katie's.

"WE'VE GOT TO FIND YOUR OWNER!" MAX DECLARED. They didn't have time to talk it over,

the sausage factory workers had called Animal Control and it was time to make a quick exit!

In the sewers, all the apartment pets had managed to escape . . .

apart from Norman, who had managed to get himself caught

in the jaws of an alligator named Derick.

"WE GOT YOUR FRIEND!"
ROARED SNOWBALL WITH DELIGHT.
"ADVANTAGE: ME!"

CANINE
Classics

Why does RIPPER chase anything red?
Because he's a **BULLDOG**!

Why did MEL put clock on his head?
He wanted to become a WATCH DOG!

What is DUKE'S favourite breakfast?
POOCHED EGGS!

Why doesn't MAX like ghost stories?
He gets too TERRIER-FIED!

Why did BUDDY go sunbathing?
He wanted to be a HOT DOG!

Why does LEONARD like bubble baths?
Because he's a SHAMPOODLE!

INSANELY
CUTE
ALSO INSANE

TM & © UNI

FUNNY FELINES!

Why was the cat afraid of the tree?
Because of its bark!

What do you call a cat with eight legs who likes to swim? **An octo-puss!**

Where does a cat buy his clothes?
A cat-alogue!

What is a cat's favourite colour?
Purrr-ple!

What is smarter than a talking cat?
A spelling bee!

What do you call a cat in the bath?
Lost.

FLUSHED RIGHT

CAN YOU HELP **SNOWBALL** FIND HIS WAY BACK TO THE FLUSHED PETS LAIR? PICK THE BEST PIPE FOR HIM TO JUMP DOWN.

A   B   C   D

TATTOO SPOT

CAN YOU FIND ALL OF TATTOO'S TATTOOS?

1

2

3

4

5

ANSWERS ON PAGE 77

Amazing PETS!

Read these totally paw-some pet facts!

Dalmatians puppies are PURE WHITE when they are born.

Dogs were the first animals to be kept by humans as PETS.

Dogs can make 100 emotional expressions with just their EARS.

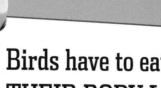

Birds have to eat HALF THEIR BODY-WEIGHT in food each day.

Goldfish can live for 40 YEARS.

Most hamsters BLINK
with one eye at a time.

Cats are amazing jumpers and can leap
up to SEVEN TIMES their own height.

A group of kittens
is called a KINDLE.

Cats have FOUR TOES on their back
paws and FIVE on their front paws.

Each nose pad of a cat is as
individual as a FINGERPRINT.

Max convinced Duke and they set off to find Duke's owners. They had lived near the sausage factory, but when the dogs approached the front door, a sneering cat called Reginald informed them that Duke's owner had died. Duke was devastated and he blamed Max for persuading him to look for his old owner.

As Max walked away from Duke he got caught by Animal Control! He thought all was lost until Duke saved him by pouncing on the Animal Control worker. Max was freed, but Duke was caught and thrown into the Animal Control van.

Meanwhile, the Flushed Pets had come up with a plan to find Max and get their revenge. They had disguised themselves as humans . . . in fact, they had disguised themselves as a mother and a baby!
Soon they saw the Animal Control van being chased by Max and the Flushed Pets managed to stop the van. The showdown between Max and Snowball began.

Even though Snowball was brave and daring, he wasn't very strong and Max was soon able to get the better of him. As they argued, Snowball noticed that Animal Control had picked up Tattoo and Dragon too. There was only one option left – Max and Snowball had to work together!

Snowball had a crazy plan to take over a bus and use it to follow the Animal Control. Max worked the pedals of the bus and Snowball steered, trying to hit as many things as he could in the process. Soon they managed to hit the Animal Control van, but both vehicles swerved and both ended up dangling off the side of a bridge!

Max rescued Snowball from the wreckage only to be faced with the rest of the Flushed Pets, who were ready to attack! Just before the Flushed Pets launched their attack, Gidget and the apartment pets appeared to rescue Max. This distraction gave Max enough time to scamper into the Animal Control van and try to rescue Duke.

As hard as he tried Max couldn't open Duke's cage and soon the van had plummeted into the water. Who could save them now? Snowball dived into the water with some of his homemade carrot keys and he managed to save everyone from the van.

Meanwhile, Tattoo had managed to find a taxi and offered to give all the pets a lift home.

Back at the apartment block, all the pets settled back into their homes, happy to be safe and back with their owners. Max thanked Gidget and she was delighted when they arranged to spend some more time together. Max, Duke and Katie had dinner together as a family. All was well – but what about Snowball? He decided that he would continue his war on humans – until he was scooped up and hugged by little girl.

Because, well, everyone wants to be loved, **RIGHT?**

TRUE
OR FALSE?

How well do you know the pets? TIME TO FIND OUT!

1
MAX'S owner is called Lucy.

TRUE   FALSE

2
DUKE came from the rescue centre.

TRUE   FALSE

3
LEONARD is a hard rock fan.

TRUE   FALSE

4
GIDGET is secretly in love with Buddy.

TRUE   FALSE

5
MEL'S best friend is a squirrel.

TRUE   FALSE

6
SWEETPEA is afraid of heights.

TRUE   FALSE

7 SNOWBALL CAN TURN CARROTS INTO KEYS.

☐ TRUE ☐ FALSE

8 THE FLUSHED PETS LIVE IN THE PARK.

☐ TRUE ☐ FALSE

9 THE INITIATION CEREMONY FOR THE FLUSHED PETS INVOLVES A VIPER.

☐ TRUE ☐ FALSE

10 TATTOO IS A GUINEA PIG.

☐ TRUE ☐ FALSE

11 SNOWBALL'S MOTTO IS "FOREVER LIBERATED, NEVER DOMESTICATED!"

☐ TRUE ☐ FALSE

12 OZONE REALLY LIKES DOGS.

☐ TRUE ☐ FALSE

ANSWERS ON PAGE 77

ANSWERS

PAGE 16
1. Chloe, **2.** Max, **3.** Sweetpea,
4. Buddy, **5.** Leonard, **6.** Gidget.

PAGE 17

PAGE 18
1. d, **2.** b, **3.** a, **4.** c.

PAGE 19
Piece **e** doesn't fit.

PAGE 24
1. Duke, **2.** Leonard, **3.** Chloe, **4.** Max, **5.** Gidget.

PAGE 27
Duke has taken over the bed.

PAGE 28

PAGE 30
Bag **k** is Gidget's Bag.

PAGE 34

PAGE 35

PAGE 36

PAGE 37

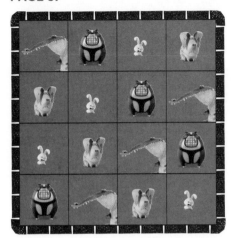

PAGE 46

PAGE 49
1. c, **2.** d, **3.** a, **4.** b.

PAGE 56
Duke should choose conveyor belt d.

PAGE 58

PAGE 59

4 is the odd tattoo Out (he is missing one earring).

PAGE 68
Pipe **B**

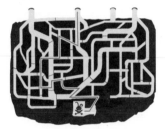

PAGE 69

PAGE 74
1. **False.** Max's owner is Katie.
2. **True.**
3. **True.**
4. **False.** Gidget is in love with Max.
5. **False.**
6. **False.**

PAGE 75
7. **True.**
8. **False.** The Flushed Pets live in the sewers.
9. **True.**
10. **False.** Tattoo is a pig.
11. **False.** Snowball's motto is "Liberated Forever. Domesticated, Never!"
12. **False.**